AF489235

mediocrobot presents...
An 8-step guide to solving the 3x3 Rubik's Cube

Intro

Welcome to this informative and fun guide for solving a standard 3x3 cube! This guide breaks up the process into 8 bite-size steps. While the guide can theoretically be read in a short timespan, it is advised that the reader spend time really getting to know each step. Each step consists of a formula or two to help you on your way. We provide some tips for memorizing these formulas, but the best way to get them to stick is through repetition.

Terminology

Before we get into the steps necessary in solving a 3x3 cube, let's break down some of the terms you'll see throughout this guide. Additionally, this section points out some basic rules / laws / constants to keep in mind.

Pieces

A standard 3x3 Rubik's cube consists of 26 total pieces, comprised of 3 types described below. Each section contains pictures of a solved cube from two different angles. Each section's specific pieces are colored in order to give you a better idea of the pieces described. For illustrative purposes, the rest of the pieces are colored light-grey (but a real cube contains no grey pieces).

Face pieces

- Count: 6
- These pieces are located in the center of each side of the cube.
- They are described by a single color.

Fig 1-1: The blue, yellow, and red faces

Fig 1-2: The orange, white, and green faces

Corner pieces

- Count: 8
- As their name suggests, these pieces are located at each corner of the cube.
- Each corner contains three colors.
- The corners can be split into groups of four "Yellow" and four "White" corners.

Fig 2-1*: The 4 yellow corners on top*

Fig 2-2*: The 4 white corners on top*

Edge pieces

- Count: 12
- This group consists of "everything else".
- As their name suggests, these pieces are located along the edge of each side, between two corner pieces.
- Each edge contains 2 colors.
- The edges can be split into groups of 4 "White", 4 "Yellow", and 4 "Middle" pieces.

Fig 3-1*: The 4 yellow edges on top*

Fig 3-2*: The 4 white edges on top*

Sides

The cube contains 6 surfaces or "sides", each containing 9 colored squares. Each center-piece, or "face", describes the color of that entire side, even if the remaining 8 tiles contain other colors (see examples below). It may surprise you to learn that the *face* of each side never actually moves, in relation to the rest of the sides. The corners and edges merely move around the face pieces.

Fig 4-1*: These are the blue, yellow, and red sides, despite the surrounding colors.*

Fig 4-2*: These are the orange, white, and green sides, despite the surrounding colors.*

Fun Fact
The opposite faces always differentiate by a factor of yellow. This means that the White face is always opposite Yellow, Blue is always opposite Green, and Red is always opposite Orange. Try it out!

Layers

There are 3 layers to a 3x3 cube. For the purposes of this lesson, we will refer to the layers as described in this section.

White Layer

The White layer is sometimes referred to as the "First" or "Bottom" layer. However, "bottom" can be misleading because the first steps in this guide describe a cube turned upside down, so the white is effectively the "top" layer in those steps. In any case, this layer consists of 9 total pieces: the 4 white corners, the 4 white edges, and the white face. A completed first layer not only contains these 9 pieces, but all 4 corners must match their adjacent edge pieces, as pictured below.

Fig 5-1: A view of the completed white layer showing the blue and red edge pieces.

Fig 5-2: A view of the completed white layer showing the orange and green edge pieces.

Middle Layer

The next layer is commonly referred to as the Middle layer or "Second" layer. It consists of 8 total pieces: the Blue, Red, Orange, and Green face pieces, plus the four edge pieces between each of those faces. A middle layer is considered completed when the middle-edge pieces match up with their adjacent faces AND the entire middle layer lines up w/ the white layer, as pictured below.

Fig 6-1: A view of the completed middle layer showing the blue and red middle pieces.

Fig 6-2: A view of the completed middle layer showing the orange and green middle pieces.

Yellow Layer

The last layer is known as the Yellow layer, and it may also be referred to as the "Top" layer or, you guessed it, the "Last" layer. Again, it's important to note that the "top" name can be misleading because sometimes the cube is turned upside down. The yellow layer consists of 9 total pieces: the 4 yellow corners, the 4 yellow edges, and the yellow face. A yellow layer is considered complete when all yellow corners match up with their adjacent edge pieces AND the yellow layer aligns with the middle and white layers on each side, as pictured below. In other words, a completed yellow layer means a completed cube!

Fig 7-1: *A view of the completed top layer showing the blue and red sides.*

Fig 7-2: *A view of the completed top layer showing the orange and green sides.*

Movements

We'll soon get into your first formulas, but let's first discuss the individual *movements* that make up those formulas. In each of the movements below, the photos will show you the state of the cube *before* and *after* the movement. The photos in this section will show you the movements as if you were holding the cube with the blue face facing you, the yellow face on top, and the red face in your right hand. However, the colors are used only to give you an idea of each movement; you can practice these movements on any side or color you wish. **Unless otherwise noted, all photos in this guide assume the user is viewing the photo from the left side.**

Each movement has its standard form, a reverse form known as the "back" movement, and the double form known as a "two" movement. That may sound complicated, but it will get easier with the following breakdowns.

Right

A "Right" twist is one performed with your right hand, twisting the right side of the cube away from you. It is abbreviated as "R" and also symbolized as R. When twisting the right side of the cube toward you, that's known as "R-Back" and symbolized as R`. Twisting the right side twice in a row in either direction is known as "R2" and symbolized as R_2.

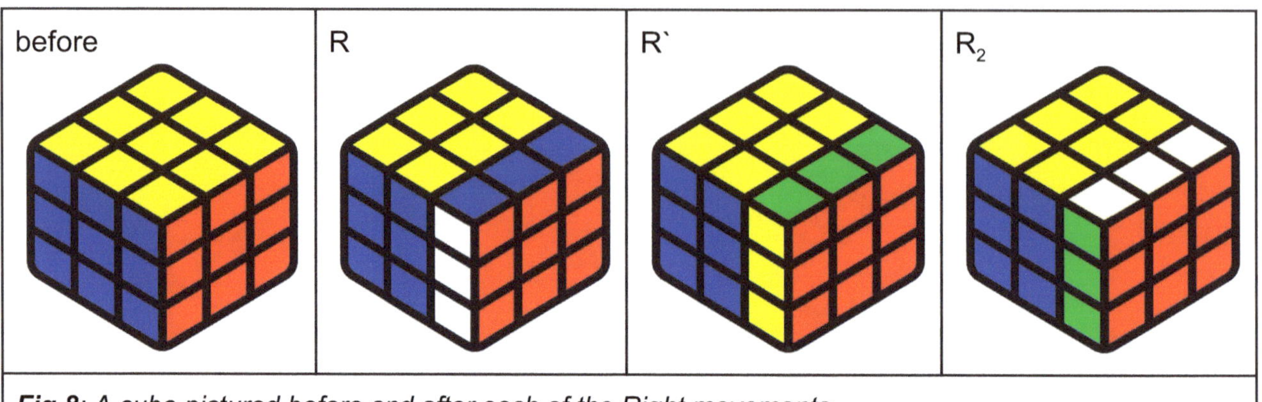

Fig 8: A cube pictured before and after each of the Right movements

Left

A "Left" twist is one performed with your left hand, twisting the left side of the cube away from you. It is abbreviated as "L" and also symbolized as L. When twisting the left side of the cube toward you, that's known as "L-Back" and symbolized as L`. Twisting the left side twice in a row in either direction is known as "L2" and symbolized as L_2.

Fig 9: A cube pictured before and after each of the Left movements

Front

A "Front" twist is one performed with either hand, taking the closest side of the cube and twisting it clockwise. It is abbreviated as "F" and also symbolized as F. When twisting the front side of the cube counter-clockwise, that's known as "F-Back" and symbolized as F`. Twisting the front side twice in a row in either direction is known as "F2" and symbolized as F_2.

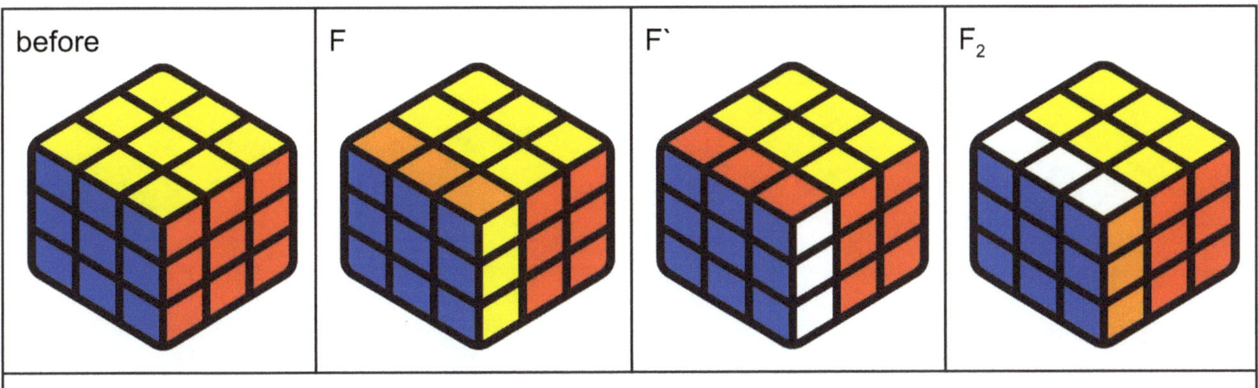

Fig 10: *A cube pictured before and after each of the Front movements*

Up

An "Up" twist is one performed with either hand, taking the top layer of the cube and twisting it clockwise. It is abbreviated as "U" and also symbolized as U. When twisting the top layer of the cube counter-clockwise, that's known as "U-Back" and symbolized as U`. Twisting the top layer twice in a row in either direction is known as "U2" and symbolized as U_2.

Fig 11: *A cube pictured before and after each of the Up movements*

Down

A "Down" twist is one performed with either hand, taking the bottom layer of the cube and twisting it clockwise. It is abbreviated as "D" and also symbolized as D. When twisting the bottom layer of the cube counter-clockwise, that's known as "D-Back" and symbolized as D`. Twisting the bottom layer twice in a row in either direction is known as "D2" and symbolized as D_2.

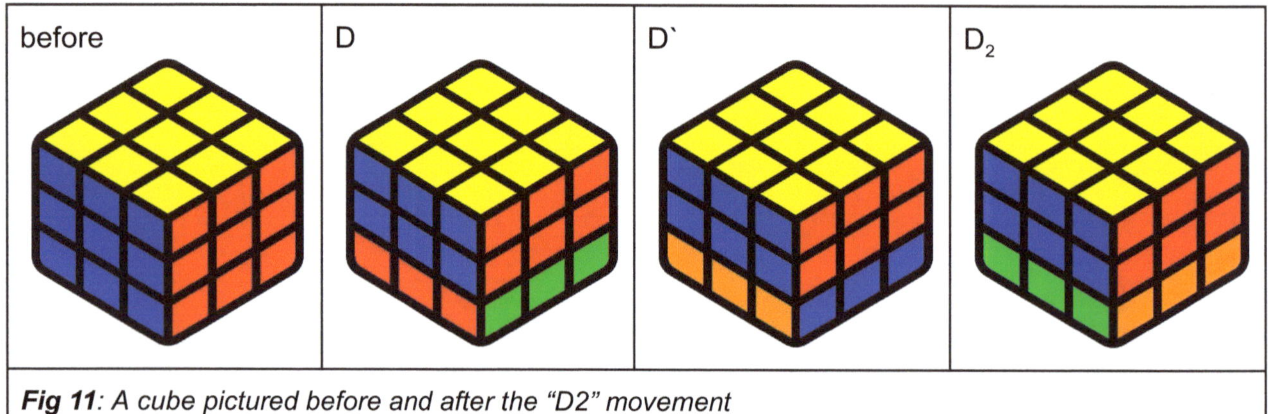

Fig 11: A cube pictured before and after the "D2" movement

Shuffling

You've probably already got shuffling down already, but it will be nice to make sure you know how to quickly and effectively shuffle your cube. After all, you'll soon be solving this thing all the time, and you'll want to be able to quickly reset to a scrambled state. One easy way is to hold the cube in your right hand with the yellow face up (1). Then, alternate performing an L twist (2), then spinning the entire cube counter-clockwise (3), and so on (4). After you've done that a random number of times, you can rotate the cube so a different face is up and keep performing those steps. Usually, a shuffle on 2 or 3 different upward-facing sides is sufficient.

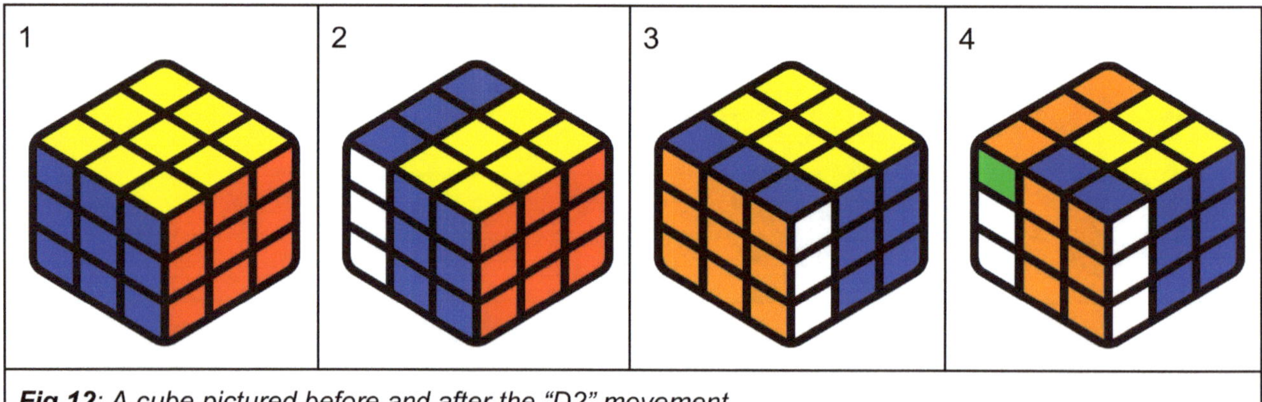

Fig 12: A cube pictured before and after the "D2" movement

The Steps

Before proceeding, make sure you're comfortable with all of the basic pieces and movements. Do you know the difference between a white face and a yellow corner? How about an R2 vs an L-Back? If not, give those another look. We won't judge. If you have the movements down, that will make it easier later to see, memorize, and utilize a formula like FURU`R`F`.

Each of the following steps may seem short, but it's important that you sit with each step and really try to learn it. That will make it easier to string together several of these steps and eventually solve a cube with nothing but that brain of yours.

Note - Some of these photos will contain red and blue pieces to help illustrate the parts of the cube we're rotating, but your cube could contain any color in these scenarios.

1 - The White Cross

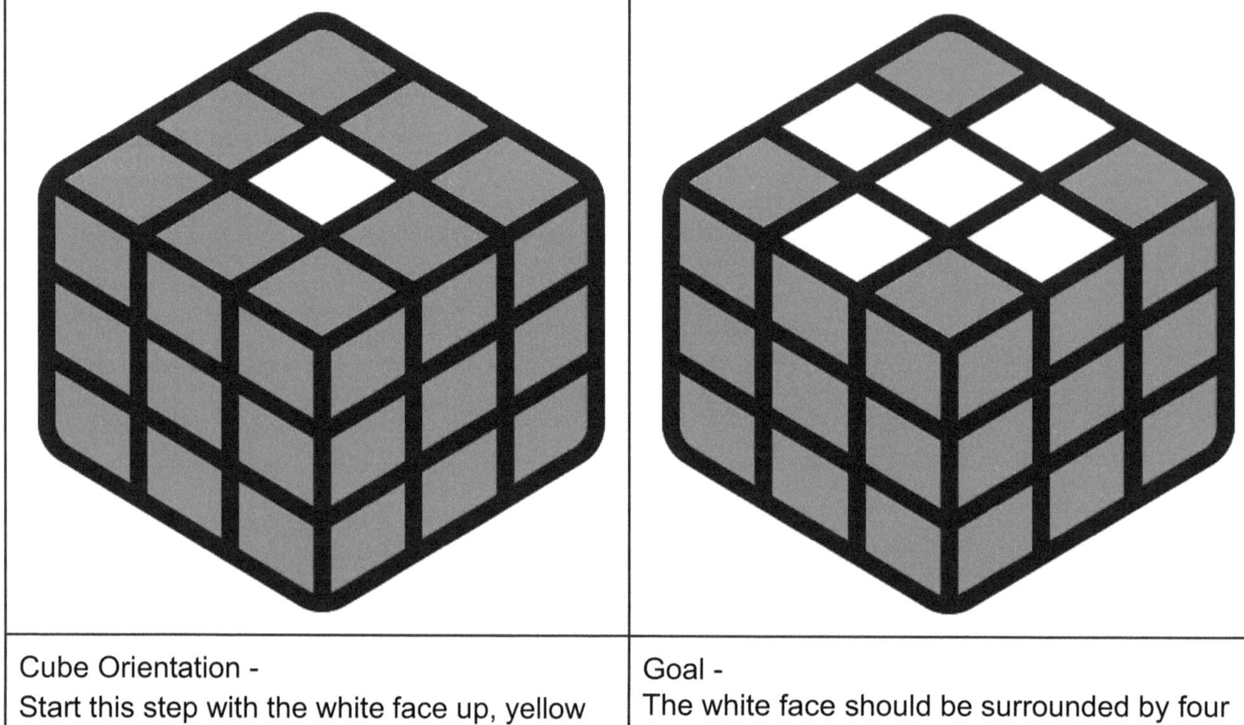

Cube Orientation - Start this step with the white face up, yellow face down.	Goal - The white face should be surrounded by four white edge pieces.

The White Cross is sometimes known as the "X" or white "Plus Sign". Unlike the rest of the steps in this guide, this first step does not involve any formulas. Instead, it involves working on your intuition and getting comfortable with the layout of the cube. Later, when more pieces are in their proper places, it becomes difficult to perform a move without "ruining" several earlier moves and scattering your earlier progress. However, that's not the case with this first step. Since the entire cube is unsolved at this point, we're able to freely move most of the cube without messing up the progress on the white cross.

The four white edge pieces can each be found in one of five possible positions. We'll cover how to get the pieces up into the cross for each of those scenarios. In some of these scenarios, we say a white edge piece is "blocked". That happens when we want to rotate the piece into the top layer, but a white edge piece is already in that spot. In those cases, we'll twist the top layer until our piece can freely move into the top layer without disturbing another white edge piece.

Scenario 1

White edge piece is already in the white layer, directly adjacent to the white face. When this happens, no further action is needed on this particular edge piece. It's already part of the white cross.

Scenario 2a

White edge piece in the middle layer, not blocked by an edge piece in the white layer (1). Simply rotate the white edge up so it touches the white face (2).

Scenario 2b

White edge piece is in the middle layer, and is blocked by an edge piece in the white layer (1). First, use a U or U` twist to rotate the top edge piece out of the way (2). Then, rotate the middle piece up into place (3).

Scenario 3

White edge piece in the white layer, facing the outside of the cube (1). Rotate this piece down 90° to the middle layer (2), and then proceed as if this edge piece were in Scenario 2.

Scenario 4a

White edge piece in the bottom row, facing the outside of the cube, not blocked by a piece in the white layer (1). Rotate this piece up 90° to the middle layer (2), and then proceed as if this edge piece were in Scenario 2.

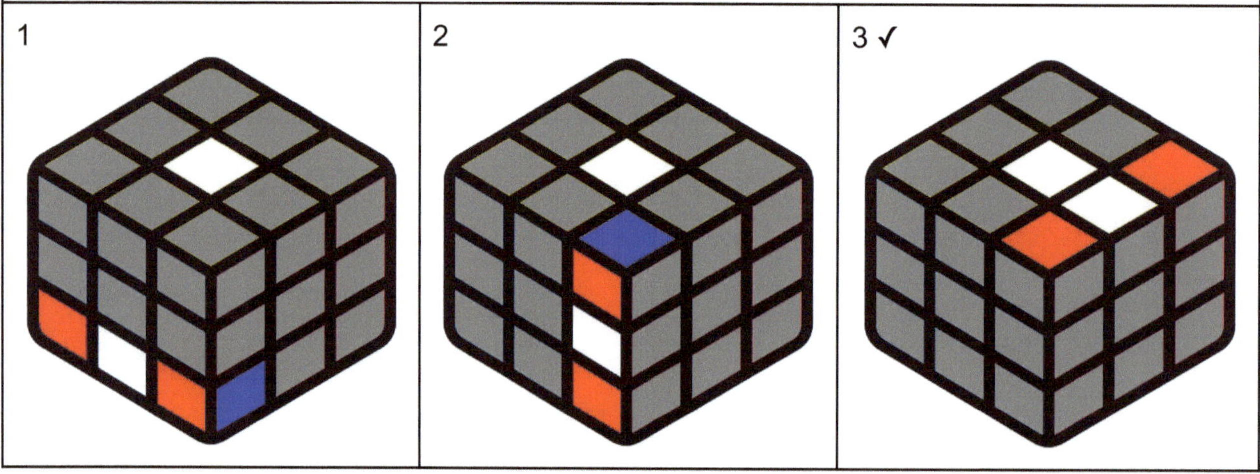

Scenario 4b

White edge piece is in the bottom layer, facing the outside of the cube, and is blocked by an edge piece in the top layer (1). First, use a U or U` twist to rotate the top edge piece out of the way (2). Then, rotate the middle piece up 90° to the middle layer (3), and then proceed as if this edge piece were in Scenario 2.

1

2

3

4 ✓

Scenario 5a

White edge piece in the bottom layer, facing the bottom of the cube, not blocked by a piece in the top layer (1). Simply rotate this piece up 180° to the top layer (2).

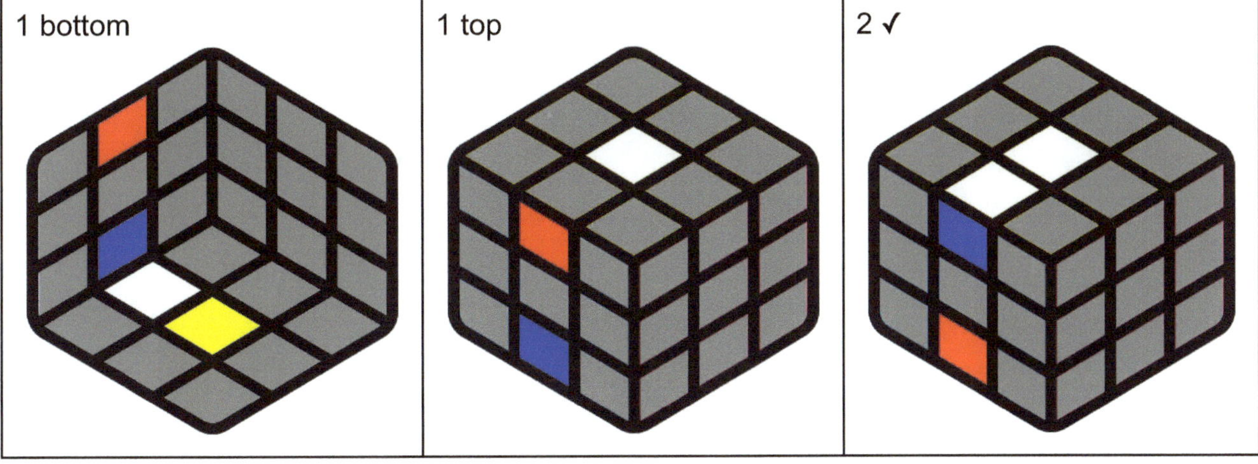

1 bottom

1 top

2 ✓

Scenario 5b

White edge piece in the bottom layer, facing the bottom of the cube, blocked by a piece in the
top layer (1). First, use a U or U` twist to get the existing white edge piece out of the way (2).
Then, rotate this bottom piece up 180° to the top layer (3).

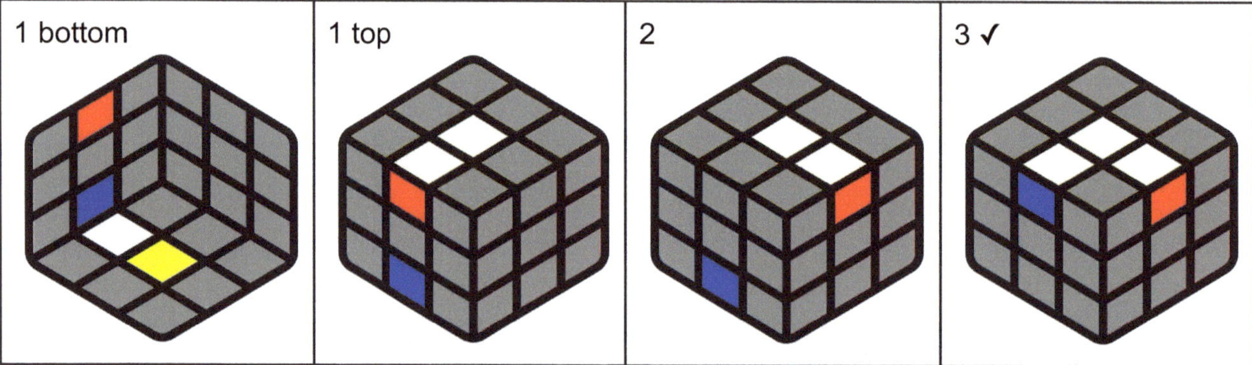

2 - The White Cross, Extended

Cube Orientation - Start this step with the white face up, yellow face down. Step 1 should be completed.	Goal - Each non-white color of the four white edges should be touching a matching face in the middle layer.

Besides Yellow and White, there are 4 more face pieces located throughout the middle layer. We want to align each of those faces with the white edge piece of the same color. So how do we get there?

First, twist the white layer as many times as needed using U or U` twists. Attempt to line-up the white edge pieces w/ the colored faces on each side of the cube. You'll be able to line-up at least two of the faces.

Similar to step 1, you'll find yourself in one of two possible scenarios, and we've got formulas to help you quickly solve either situation. Actually, there is a third scenario, where you're required to do nothing. Let's cover that one first.

Scenario 1

Middle pieces are already aligned with the white edge pieces. When this happens, no further action is needed. Our extended white cross is already complete.

Scenario 2 - Setup

Two bad faces are on opposite sides of the cube. Position the cube so the "bad" edges are on the left and right sides of the cube.

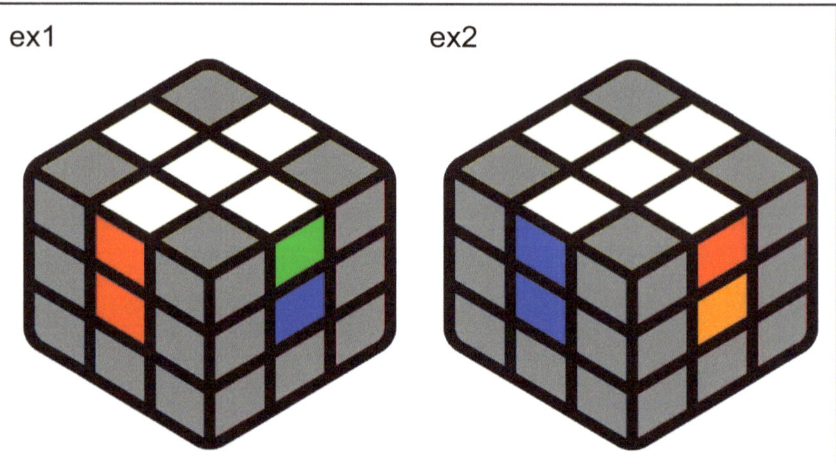

Scenario 2 - Formula

Formula - $L_2R_2D_2L_2R_2$
Summary - Perform the L2 and R2 twists to temporarily send your two bad white edges down to the yellow layer (1). Then, perform a D2 twist to align the bad white edges with the proper middle faces (2). Finally, perform L2 and R2 again to send the white faces back up to the white layer (3).

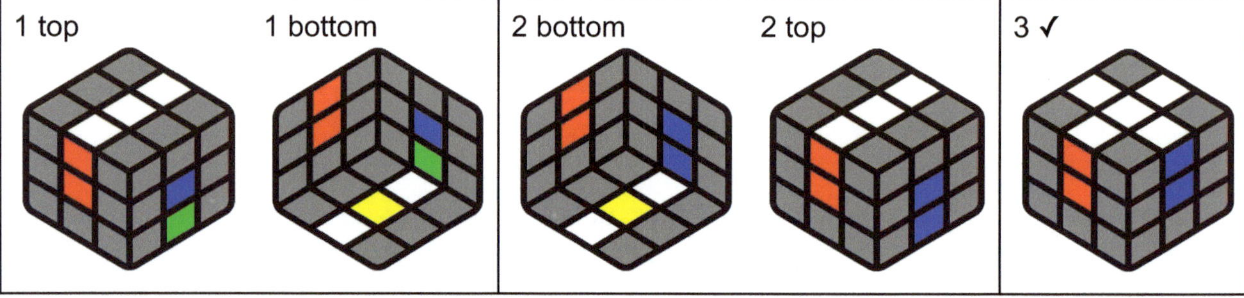

Scenario 3 - Setup

Two bad faces are on adjacent sides of the cube. Position the cube so the "bad" edges are on the front (closest side) and right sides of the cube.

ex1   ex2

Scenario 3 - Formula

Formula - $R_2DF_2D`R_2$

Summary - Perform an R2 twist to send one of the bad white edges down to the yellow layer (1). Rotate the bottom layer w/ a D twist to align this bad white edge underneath its proper middle face (2). Next, perform an F2 twist to send a white edge up to the top layer while sending the remaining bad white edge down to the bottom layer (3). Finally, perform D` to shift the remaining bad white edge underneath its matching middle face (4), followed by R2 to send that white edge back up to the top layer (5).

1	2	3	4	5 ✓

3 - White Corners

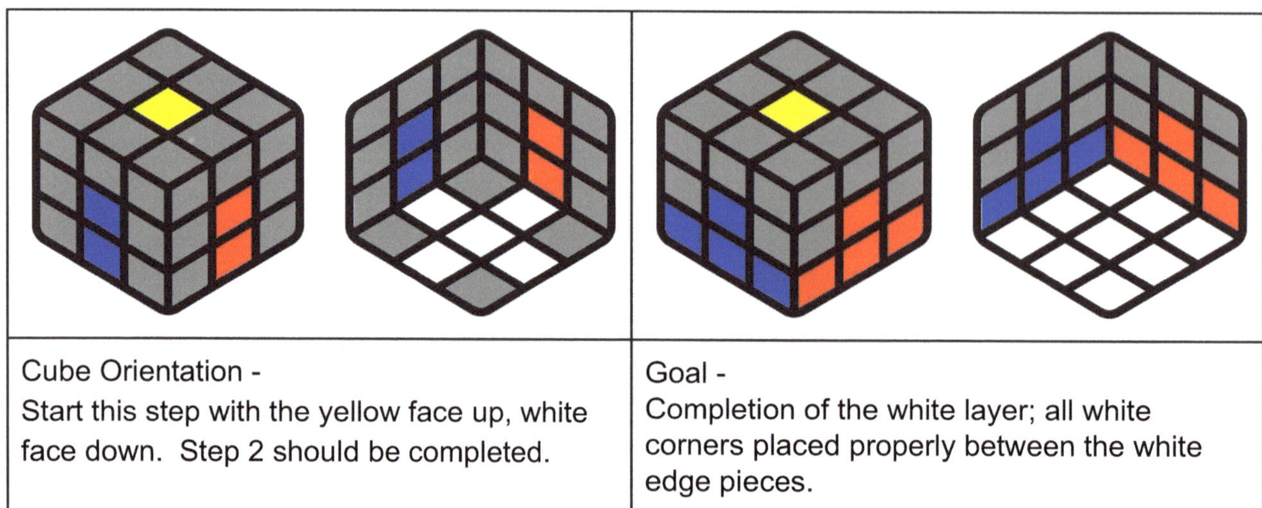

Cube Orientation - Start this step with the yellow face up, white face down. Step 2 should be completed.	Goal - Completion of the white layer; all white corners placed properly between the white edge pieces.

The first step here is to locate each white corner in the yellow layer and perform U or U` twists until the corner is located between the other two colors of the corner piece. In other words, if you're working on the red-and-blue white corner, you'll want to twist the yellow layer until this corner piece is between the red and blue faces (see pictures below). Then, hold the cube so that the white corner is located in the top, left, closest corner to you.

Possible scenarios include the corner with white tile facing Left (1), Front (2), or Up (3). There is also a fourth scenario in which the white corner is not located in the yellow layer at all (4), and we'll cover that as well. Note, for this White Corners section, **the pictures are shown as if you're viewing the cube from the right;** the red face in these pictures. This will make it easier to view the scenarios.

Scenario 1

The corner's white tile is facing left. The formula for this step is LU`L`. Moving forward, we'll start showing fewer pictures related to each individual movement, but for now, here are photos shown before this formula, followed by the L, U`, and L` movements.

Scenario 2

The corner's white tile is facing you (ie - facing the "front"). The formula for this step is U`LUL`. The below photos show you how the cube should look after performing the U`, LU, and L` steps. Notice how the third and fourth pictures match in scenarios 1 and 2.

Scenario 3

The corner's white tile is facing up. The formula for this step is LU₂L`ULU`L`.  Now, that might seem like a long formula, so it may be easier to think of this as LU₂L`U, followed by the formula from Scenario 1. In other words, after performing LU₂L`U, the white tile will be facing left, and you already know how to solve for that.  The below photos show you how the cube should look after performing the LU₂, L'U, and LU'L` steps.

Scenario 4

The white corner is down in the white layer, but it's facing the wrong direction or it's between the wrong edge pieces. When this happens, hold the cube so that this "bad" corner is located in the bottom, lefthand corner closest to you (see examples below). Next, perform the formula LU`L` to pop the corner up into the yellow layer. You are now in one of the scenarios 1 through 3, so refer to those sections above.

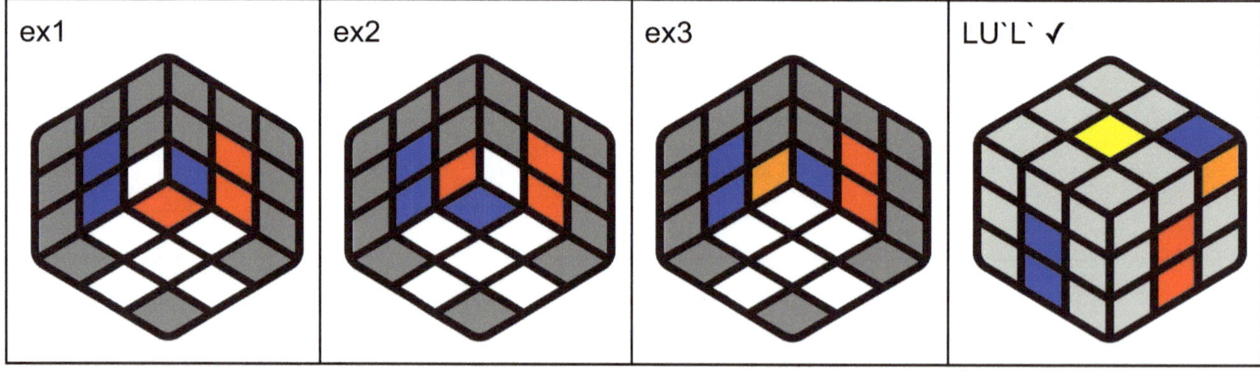

4 - Middle Edges

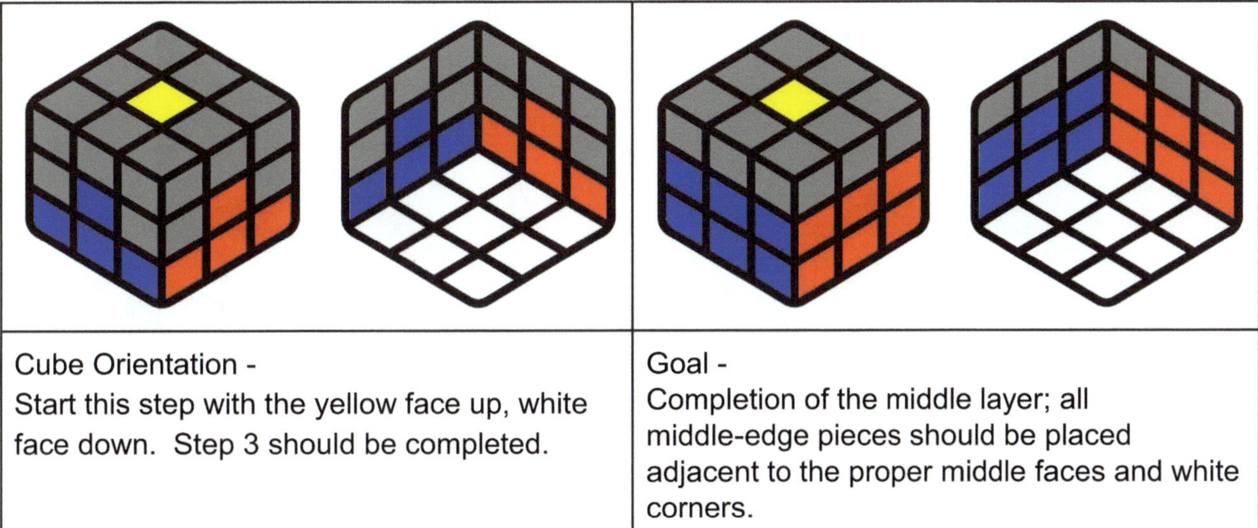

Cube Orientation - Start this step with the yellow face up, white face down. Step 3 should be completed.	Goal - Completion of the middle layer; all middle-edge pieces should be placed adjacent to the proper middle faces and white corners.

This step involves putting the 4 non-white, non-yellow, edge pieces into their proper spots in the middle layer. There are primarily two scenarios for this step. However, like step 3, there is an extra scenario possible where you'll need to perform an extra couple of moves to get your piece into one of the two main situations.

Now, scenarios 1 and 2 are very similar, and their formulas are similar as well. In fact, the formulas are identical, except they involve movements in opposite directions Both situations involve you locating a non-yellow edge piece in your yellow layer. Start by rotating the top layer until a desired edge piece is touching the same color of a middle-layer face. Then, hold the cube so this edge piece (and its matching middle-layer face) are in your right hand; see photos below. At that point, the edge piece will either need to be rotated one of two ways; toward you (1) or away from you (2). Note - in this section, we're back to showing you views from the left side.

Scenario 1 - Setup

Edge piece in yellow layer needs to be moved into the middle layer towards you.

Scenario 2 - Setup

Edge piece in yellow layer needs to be moved into the middle layer away from you.

Scenario 1 - Formula

Formula - R`U`R`U`R`, URUR
Summary - This formula seems long, but it's really just 5 twists in one direction, followed by 4 more twists in the opposite direction. Over time, that will be the main thing you memorize for this step; you'll count to 5 during each of those "back" movements, and then count to 4 during the remaining forward movements.

before

after

Scenario 2 - Formula

Formula - RURUR, U`R`U`R`
Summary - Again, this seemingly long formula is really just 5 twists in one direction, followed by 4 more twists in the opposite direction. Like scenario 1, you'll get to the point where you'll count to 5 during each of those initial forward movements, and then count to 4 during the remaining "back" movements.

before

after

Scenario 3

A non-yellow edge piece is already in the middle layer, but it's facing the wrong direction or it's the wrong color entirely. In those cases, position a yellow piece in the yellow layer, and rotate it down into place using the formulas from Scenario 1 or 2.

In example 2 below, the red-blue edge is facing the wrong direction, so the yellow-orange piece is sent to the middle layer using the Scenario 1 forumula. From that point, the blue-red piece can be lined up w/ the blue face (3) and put in its proper place using the Scenario 2 formula.

5 - Yellow Cross

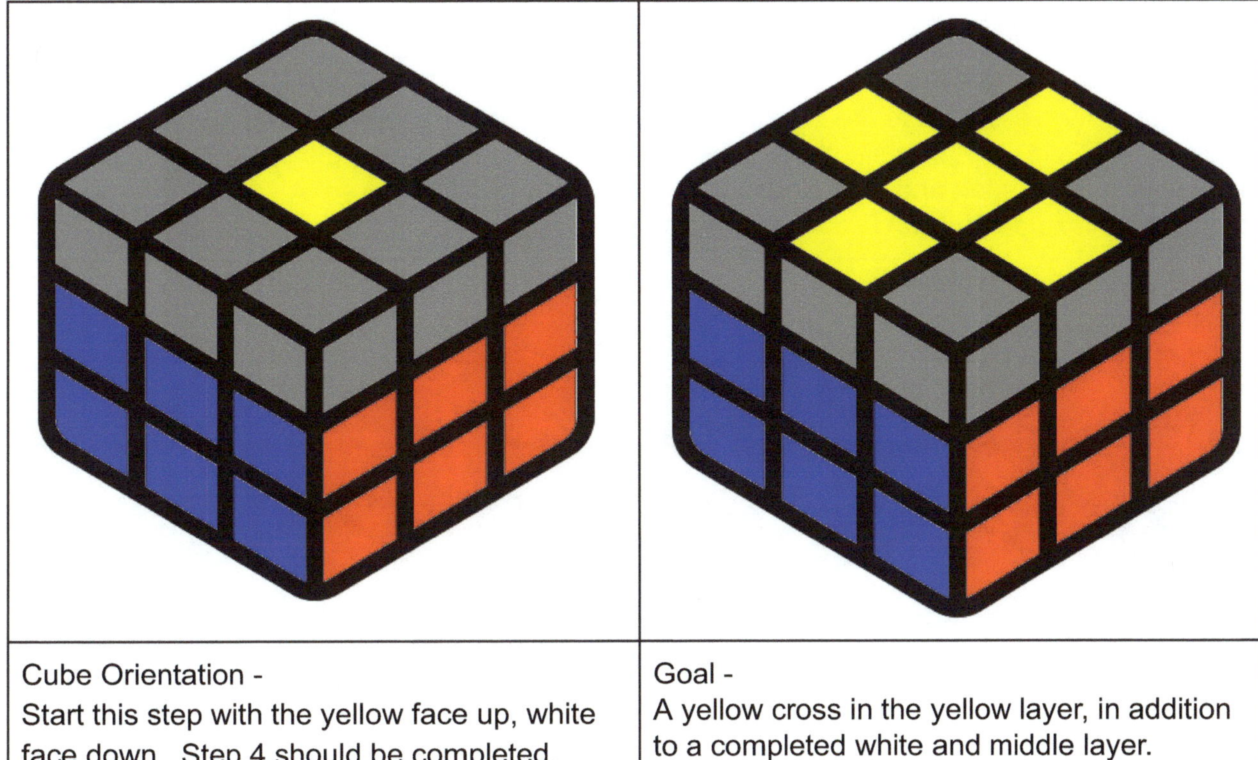

Cube Orientation - Start this step with the yellow face up, white face down. Step 4 should be completed.	Goal - A yellow cross in the yellow layer, in addition to a completed white and middle layer.

This step involves creating a Yellow cross on the top/yellow layer of the cube. There are two main scenarios for this step and, like step 4, the formulas are similar to one another. There's also a third scenario that's very similar to the first two, and we'll cover that as well. Technically, a fourth scenario exists where the yellow cross is already completed, but you'll know that one when you see it (and just in case you don't, refer to the "Goal" photo above).

Both of the main scenario formulas involve an F twist, then an R/U step, an opposite R/U step, followed finally by an F` twist. One way to remember these formulas is "Are you Opposite?" and "You are Adjacent". Let's explain that.

Scenario 1

Two legs of the yellow cross are in place, and they're opposite one another. The formula for this step is FRU,R`U`F`.  Position the cube so that the existing yellow pieces in the top layer are located on your left and right sides (1).  Start w/ an F twist, followed by RU, as-in "Are you opposite".  Next, perform R'U', followed finally by F`.

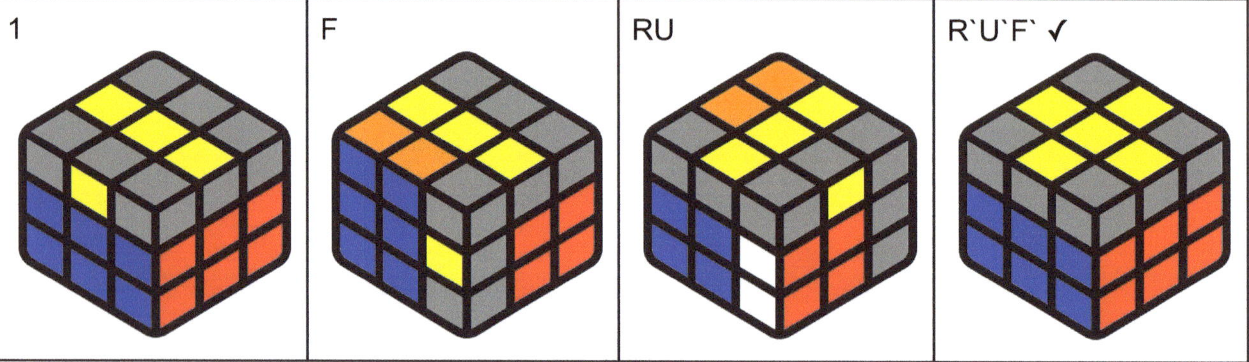

Scenario 2

Two legs of the yellow cross are in place, and they're adjacent to one another. The formula for this step is FUR,U`R`F`.  Position the cube so that the existing yellow pieces in the top layer are located on your left and furthest-away sides (1).  Start w/ an F twist, followed by UR, as-in "You are adjacent".  Next, perform U`R`, followed finally by F`.

Scenario 3

No legs of the yellow cross are in place. In this case, you can position the cube however you want (as long as the yellow face remains on top). Then, perform either of the formulas from scenario 1 or 2. This will move two yellow edges into their desired spots in the yellow level. From there, simply perform the appropriate formula from scenario 1 or 2, and you're done!

6 - Yellow Corners I

Cube Orientation -	Goal -
Start this step with the yellow face up, white face down. Step 5 should be completed.	The yellow layer contains all 9 yellow pieces, and their yellow tiles are all facing up (1). Note - it's not yet important that the other colors in the top layer line up (2).

The first part of this step involves getting the tiles into a "Fish" formation in the yellow layer, pictured below. We'll cover how to get there in a moment. The two formations seem identical at a glance, but it's important to note which direction the non-fish yellow tiles are facing. Note - The photos in this section will all be shown from directly overhead, as if you're staring down on the cube from overhead.

Fish 1

The fish is facing up and to the left, while the bottom, right-hand piece has a yellow tile facing right. Perhaps your cube *almost* looks like this, except the bottom, right-hand piece has a yellow tile facing down towards you. In that case, you have Fish 2, and you should rotate the cube 180°.

Formula: R`U`RU` R`U$_2$R (aka Fish1 Formula)

Fish 2

The fish is facing down and to the right, while the top, left-hand piece has a yellow tile facing away from you. Perhaps your cube *almost* looks like this, except the top, left-hand piece has a yellow tile facing left. In that case, you have Fish 1, and you should rotate the cube 180°.

Formula: R`U$_2$R UR`UR (aka Fish2 Formula)

The two formulas used throughout this step are really just the same formula with movements in opposite directions. One way to keep them memorized is to note that they both contain the sequence R`U$_2$R (pronounced R-Back U2 R). Formula one ends with that sequence, while formula 2 begins with it.

Scenarios

The yellow tiles of your cube will be arranged in 1 of 8 ways. We'll cover them all below, but let's summarize first. If your cube is already showing 9 yellow tiles, you can move onto step 7. If your cube shows either of the Fish patterns we described, then you'll have a single formula to perform. For the remaining 5 scenarios, you'll need to perform one of the two formulas in order to get the tiles into a Fish formation. From there, you'll perform a *second* fish formula to complete this step.

Before	Formula	After	Before	Formula	After
	(none) →			1 →	
	1 →			2 →	
	2 →			1 →	
	1 →			2 →	

7 - Yellow Corners II

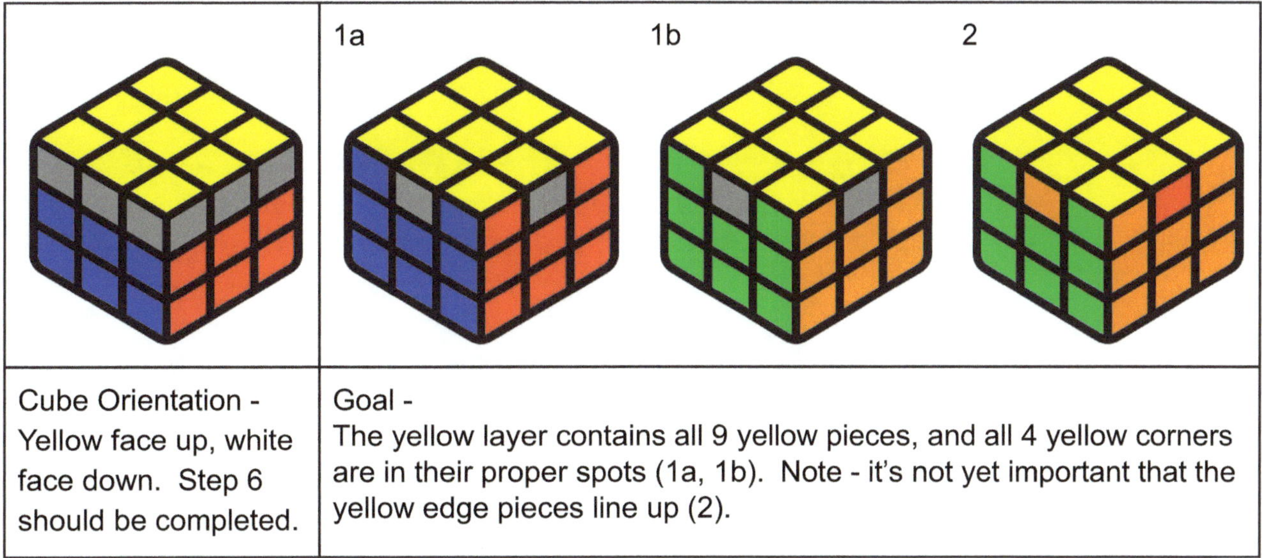

Cube Orientation - Yellow face up, white face down. Step 6 should be completed.	**Goal -** The yellow layer contains all 9 yellow pieces, and all 4 yellow corners are in their proper spots (1a, 1b). Note - it's not yet important that the yellow edge pieces line up (2).

This step comes with good news and bad news. The good news is there's only one formula to learn and the scenarios are straightforward. The bad news is the formula is quite long, but we'll work on that in a minute.

Setup

To determine which scenario you're in, twist the yellow layer as many times as you like, trying to line up two same-colored corners on the same side as their middle face piece. In the example below, we see two blue-colored corners in the top layer. A U-twist aligns the blue corners properly on the blue side of the cube (1). That's a good start, even if the other two corners are still incorrect (2).

If all four of the corners are in their proper place, move onto step 8. If not, that means that you've either got *two* good corners or *zero* good corners. If you've got zero good corners, that's okay; you'll just need to perform the below formula twice.

Formula - Background

The formula for this step is: R2D2 RUR` D2RU`R . Again, this formula seems long. We recommend breaking it up into a few sections. Perhaps you can pretend that you're a pirate talking to a robot and asking for their whereabouts like, "R2D2, are you r-back? D2, are you back? Aaargh".

In any case, you'll first want to make sure you're holding the cube the right way. Refer to the pictures below. **Note - these pictures are shown as if you're looking at the cube from the right.**

Formula - Execution

Hold the cube so the two bad corners are on the left side of the cube (1). Then, rotate the entire cube away from you so that the white face is facing you (2). Next, perform this step's formula!

After the formula, rotate the entire cube back down so the yellow face is facing up (3). Finally, twist the yellow layer until all four yellow corners line up properly with the middle layer. Note, if all 4 corners are not yet in the right position, simply work through this *Execution* section a second time.

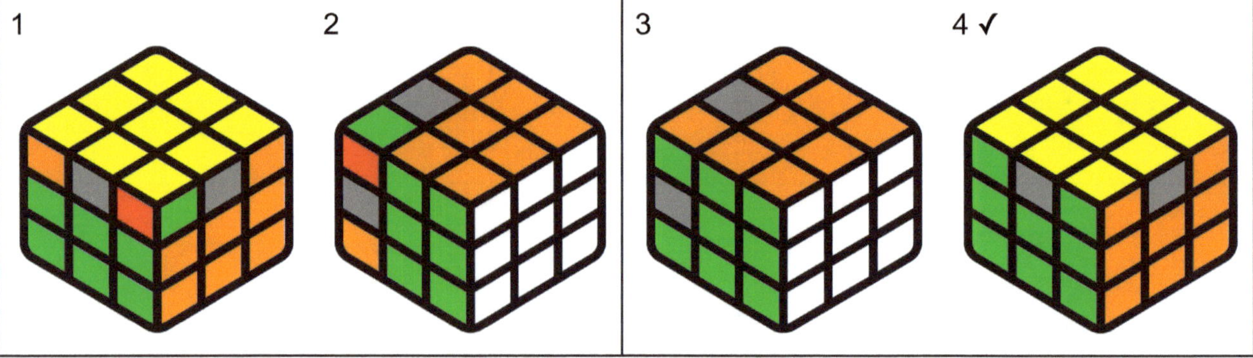

8 - Yellow Centers

You've reached the final step! We hope you're as excited as we are. Similar to the many steps we've already covered, this last step involves a couple scenarios, and a couple of nearly-identical formulas for those situations. Scenarios 1 and 2, covered below, each involve shifting three of the four yellow edges in a circular motion, while leaving one edge piece in its proper place.

However, if *none* of the yellow edge pieces are in its proper place, you'll just need to perform this step twice. Of course, if *all* of the yellow edge pieces are already in place, then you're done! **Note, the pictures in this section are shown from overhead.** The bottom of each photo is the side closest to you. Also, if the formulas seem a little daunting, check the "Formula - Expanded" section for some additional help.

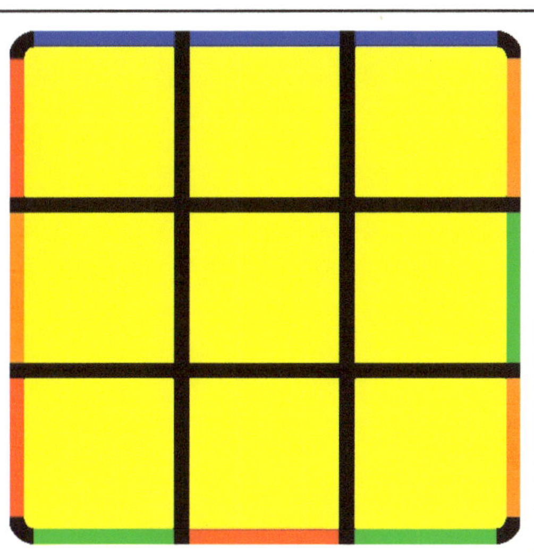

Scenario 1

Three of the four yellow edge pieces are in the wrong spot, and they need to shift in a clockwise direction. Hold the cube so the good edge is furthest from you (the blue side in this example).

In this example, orange, green, and red center tiles all need to shift in a clockwise pattern.

Formula: F_2 U L`R`F_2LR U F_2

Scenario 2

Three of the four yellow edge pieces are in the wrong spot, and they need to shift in a counter-clockwise direction. Hold the cube so the good edge is furthest from you (the blue side in this example).

In this example, green, orange, and red center tiles all need to shift in a counter-clockwise pattern.

Formula: F_2 U` L`R`$F_2$LR U` F_2

Scenario 3

All four yellow edge pieces are in the wrong spot. It doesn't matter which edge is furthest from you, and you can use either formula.

Once you're done executing one of the above formulas, you'll have one good edge piece. You're almost done, so move to scenario 1 or 2 and finish the cube!

Formula - Expanded

Let's talk a little bit more about the two formulas from this section. For starters, they're identical except for the U or U` moves. Scenario 1 uses clockwise U twists to shift the tiles clockwise. Scenario 2, on the other hand, uses counter-clockwise U-Back twists because… well, you already know why.

We'll break down the scenario 1 formula with some photos below. However, the scenario 2 formula would be the same except for a couple of U-Back twists. Note - in the example photos that follow, the red face is closest to you, and the blue face is furthest away.

Hold the cube so the good edge is furthest from you (1). Twist the front face 180° with an F2 twist, and then rotate the top layer clockwise with a U twist. Next, bring both sides of the cube down towards you with L` and R` moves.

Twist the front face 180° with another F2 twist, and then send the front sides back up to the top of the cube with L and R moves. Next, perform another U twist on the top layer, before finally twisting that front face 180° one last time.

Conclusion

You're done! If you're wondering what your next steps are, try solving it again, and then again and again. The cool thing about a cube is it's (statistically) never the same puzzle twice, but you can apply these same techniques to crack the numerous versions of this puzzle over and over again.

Got questions for us? Shoot us an email at mediocrobot@gmail.com , or hit us up on social media.

Disclaimers

Cube icons inspired by - https://www.flaticon.com/authors/freepik .
Social media icons courtesy of - https://www.flaticon.com/authors/pixel-perfect and
https://www.iconfinder.com/mattbadal .
The term *Rubik's Cube* is a trademark of Ideal Toy Corporation, Hollis, New York.

Copyright notice